From A-Z: Animals Get Funky!

From A-Z: Animals Get Funky!
Published by Serendipitous Entertainment © 2017
Text © 2017 by Sarahndipity Johnsen
Illustrations © 2017 by Amanda Maitri and Sarahndipity Johnsen
Photography by Heather Redding
Graphic Design by M. Noel Daugherty
Editing by Mary Greene

Serendipitous Entertainment
First Edition, 2017
ISBN: 978-0-9993661-1-0
Library of Congress Cataloging-in-Publication Data Available
Printed in PRC
www.followyourdelight.com

From A-Z: Animals Get Funky!

SERENDIPITOUS ENTERTAINMENT

Thank You

This lyrical children's book playfully illustrates creative dance moves that support health, confidence, inclusion, and unique expression.
It's fun for mind, spirit, and body.
Inspired by Anne Green Gilbert's Dance Concepts and the work of modern dance pioneer, Rudolf von Laban, each page has been carefully crafted to highlight dance moves that support brain development, reduce stress, and inspire confident, healthy families.

This book is dedicated to all beings who dare to DREAM BIG and boldly leap when opportunities present themselves. Your smiles ripple outward and inspire others.
This dance is for you!

None of this would be possible without the support of my beautiful mother,
Debra McNees, and my loving husband, Justin Johnsen.
Thank you for always believing in me, supporting my wild dreams, and letting me fly.

Deep gratitude also goes out to an incredible community of artists and believers.
Anne Green Gilbert; Pryor, Emerson, Owens, Hope, and Finn Gilbert; Kaija and Calder Houck; Michelle and Kiana Polk; Jenny, Evan, and Eloise Lucille Ward; Heidi and Will Bassignani; Siobhan Mohr; Cathy Mooney; Zach, Louisa, Ian, and Estelle Jaehn; Linda and Alan Mullenbach; Whitney Lucille; Noelani Von Stocken; Bob and Val Hodgetts; Stephanie, Weston, and Landon Woodward; Gwendolyn, Alvin, and Sage Sessions; Peggy Wold; Jamie, Kevin, and Reegan Mahoney; Chad, Alesia, Avery Marie, and Cora June Jacobsen; Jessica and Marli Downing-Ford; Eli Rubick; Mary, Celestine, Eilis, and Alastriona; Bella, Addison, Liam, Samuel, Robyn, Lakyn, Donovan, and Logan;
Lisa Wimberger; Anam Cara Cat,
and every single heart that supported this publishing process.

Alpaca Alignment

From a solid base
stand in *PLACE*

Breathe deep
put a smile on your face

Alpaca Alignment
straight and true

The magic of dance
is waiting for you

Baboon Booty Bounce

With a baboon shaka-laka
you can announce

That you have found your *RHYTHM*
as you Booty Bounce

From your head to your tail
don't dare waste an ounce

Of that hip-shakin', Earth-quakin'
Booty Bounce

Turn yourself around and
shake that funky booty

It's a boogie dance where
EVERYONE'S A BEAUTY

Chimpanzee Conga

Travel to Salonga
Chimpanzees dance Conga
Congo through Bandundu
With friends, you can do it too
Yep, let them show you how
Step 1, 2, 3 and kick now
Hands on waist, move
through SPACE
1, 2, 3 kick in place
Down there in Salonga
Chimpanzees love Conga

Disco Dragon

Raise your fist high up into the sky now
Finger to the Moon

Curve it on down, bump it round, or Hustle
Bustle through the room

Roll those arms round each other for fun and
Robot, slow-bot swoon

YMCA SHAPES, Funky Chicken Dance
Disco Dragon Tune

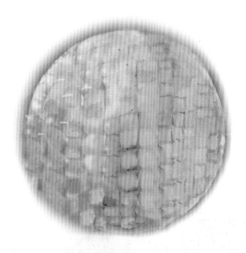

It's not the SIZE of your dance feet
But how you move, groove with the beat
With your own style, you're a bright star
Free to be you, all of us are
Electro-Trance Elephant Dance, make your own dream
Electro-Trance Elephant Dance, wake, smile, and beam
Big, small, soft, bright, or in-between
You shine your light, be the
King or Queen

Electro-Trance
Elephant Dance

There's no Hocus Pocus
Flamingo's got FOCUS
Balanced agility
Eyes track one thing to see
Just use your EYES to look
Up, down, you've got the hook
Left to right, yours to see
All that you want to be
Round and round, loop de loop
You're not a nincompoop
Those eyes what can they see?
Different ways to be free?
There's no Hocus Pocus
Flamingo's got FOCUS
Balanced agility
With healthy eyes
now you'll
SEE

Flamingo Focus

Giraffe Get Down

First you dip it down LOW

Giraffe Get DOWN

NOW other side you go
GIRAFFE Get Down

Swerve right through the middle
Bring it on up

Swerve left through the middle
Bring it on up

LEVEL
Hands to the sky
Raise up that roof

You know why you're so fly?
Here's living proof

Hip-Hop Hippopotamus

Savor the Now, it's TIME
to relax and unwind
With your body there are fun
sounds to make and find
Can you feel the rhythm
of your body drumbeat?
As you clap, slap, slap, tap, tap
and then stomp your feet?
Body Percussion uses your
hands to keep TIME
And your face as the bass
feeling infinite rhyme
The world's a jungle for
Hip-Hop Hippopotamus
With nonstop, beat-drop,
Hip-Hop for the lot of us

Iguana Improvisation

From head to toe, this is the flow
I wanna chance, Iguana Dance
Improv light touch, wakes up so much
Squeeze, tap, slap, brush, all *PARTS*, no rush
First it's a squeeze
From head past knees
Next it's a tap
Around like that
Now gently slap
Make your bod clap
Last is the brush
No need to rush
Squeeze
Tap
Slap
Brush

Jackrabbit Jump

Colorado
Rocky Mountains
up there so high
Jump up, up and
over those peaks
Learn how to fly
   Be kind to EVERYONE on Earth
      Don't you know why?

         If you JUMP'N
            You fall DOWN

            then friends won't pass you by
               We can lift each other up now
                  Hop, skip, jump spry
               Colorado
                     RABBIT
               JACK   **JUMP**
                           Give it a try

Kangaroo Kung Fu

Yo!
Kangaroo Kung Fu Master
Kick in front with
hands push-blaster
Plant your feet firm
hands at your side
Balance now and
keep your stance wide
Other DIRECTION
now you go
Kick to the back
with even flow
From Tasmania
to China
Kung Fu side-kick
hands beside ya
It's as easy as 1, 2, 3
with time, patience,
and energy

Even you
Oh Kung Fu Master
can move slow or go
much faster

Llama Limbo

How low can you go?
Llama Limbo
Touch your toes to get ready to flow
Now stand up STRAIGHT
And bend back slow

STRETCH
with your back and
bend it on down
See how far before
you hit the ground

Will you astound
and be Limbo crowned?

Monkey Mind

If your Monkey Mind
WEIGHS
heavy thoughts
that won't go away
Lift them up
and out and
then start to sway
If Tension's in
your body and
you tighten up like clay
Then INHALE
RELEASE and SOFTEN
Now, you're
ready to play
EXHALE
Notice the difference
of each and every way
BREATHE
when you are worried
Lighten up
Let it wash away

Nighthawk Ninja

SMOOTH and sneaky
Blocks many a move, lands sleekly
First here, now disappeared from sight
Force seer thou persevered, come sprite!
All you do is fluidly glide, a soul's beauty is shrewdly spied
Spread your wings, take bravely to flight,
and soar rings, break suavely through night

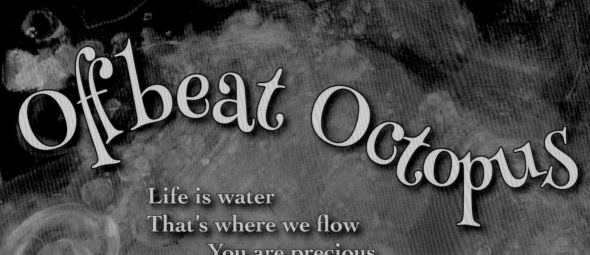

Offbeat Octopus

Life is water
That's where we flow
You are precious
In light you glow
Arms and legs are
your tentacles
Healthy oceans
bring festivals
As you hydrate,
please celebrate
Water's
Teammate,
You'll feel
so great
Offbeat Octo
BALANCE
the world
Offbeat Octo
DANCE,
FLOAT, and SWIRL

Porcupine Poke

Sometimes porcupines are thought to be quite prickly
Judgment leads to being mean and acting poorly
When other's thoughts are different, bend and
TWIST Don't **BREAK**

Stand firm in who you are and together create
Porcupines have soft quills when relaxed and themselves
Be flexible in your movements and strong in yourself
Don't let other   people's opinions get you low
Rise, stretch,   wiggle, and giggle
                                                  CONFIDENT
                                                    that you know

Quickstep Quail

There's a Quickstep Quail inside thee
Of syncopated variety

An extremely march stepping kind
One foot then 2 feet right behind

Use your energy and know-how
Move SHARP, fast as you can go now

Wobble a lot, shake that top knot
Move in an on, then offbeat, trot

You're a force to be reckoned with
Spiral, jig, and celebrate your gift

Rockin' Racoon

Hey, what instruments do you play?
Raccoon kits rock the night away

Instruments bring fascination
Use your vast imagination

Cast yourself in the leading role
Bebop, Hip-Hop, or Rock n' Roll

Harmonize a group sensation
Come together fission-fusion

Mutually loving friendships are
Symbiotic RELATIONSHIPS

Rockin' your roll alone is fine
But together, it's masterpiece time

Sloth Swagger

Sloths may be quite slow
But they're confident in the way they roll

Sloths' got   some slow strut SWAGGER
When they   slide, slip, swing, and stagger

Spread   arms wide, ready for a hug

Cross legs tight, nice and snug

Now plant legs wide on the ground
Cross arms, hug yourself nice and sound

Rock side-to-side and front-to-back
Self-love hugs are where it's at

Whether shy or a bragger
Be surefooted in your Sloth Swagger

SPIN and then you twist Turtle Turn around
Right like a clock, flip your feet to the sound

Then to the left to whirl and have some fun
Twirl with your arms spread out wide like the sun

Now plant your feet and focus on your crown
Swing back-and-forth with your head upside down

Let your arms flow, letting go side-to-side
Turtle Turn is a funky wild ride

Turtle Turn

Unique Unicorn

You're like a Unique Unicorn
One-of-a-kind gift to adorn

With moves, grace, and
FLOW united
You're a force that's unrepeated

So smoothly skilled and notable
Your choices are remarkable

That fresh style is distinctive
The inclusive flair instinctive

Knack for the imaginary
Makes your life EXTRAORDINARY

Perfect rare gem, that's what you are
Keep being you, and you'll go far!

Viper Veer

Camouflaged in the Costa Rican jungle
Vipers appear
Breathe, release Fear
REPEAT, release Fear
Learn to Veer, Viper Veer
Stretch lower limbs as you migrate
Slowly, legs only, arms straight
Slither, slide, twist, or oscillate
Lower body moves feel great
Now your hands tell their tale
Snake, slip super slowly
like a snail

Ground your feet, let your arms unveil
Secret worlds where you prevail
You can do it, lickety split
Use your top or bottom bit
As you dance, you'll be fit
To flourish in your fearless spirit

Wallaby Wiggle

Unlock the riddle, learn Wallaby wiggle
It's a jiggle, wriggle, squiggle, and giggle

Choose FAST, s l o w, or keep it right in the middle
But why doddle your PACE even a little?

Up down jiggle, side-to-side triple wriggle,
LOOP, curl, squiggle, twist and turn tickle- giggle

Let the mind boggle and the body woggle
Get up and do it, no lazy boondoggle

Up down jiggle, side-to-side triple wriggle,
LOOP, curl, squiggle, twist and turn tickle- giggle

Xenoceratops
X-RAY

Take a good look
Your body's a book

Now here's the way
Stand in X-Ray

Just use your right
Close your book tight

Open it now
Just right somehow

Then your left side
Close now from wide

Open again
Left, right, you win

CONTRAST at last
Having a blast

YETI YAWN

Yeti Yawns start SMALL from within
Tight like a ball with only kin

Earthbound friends shift in the background
Safe, sound, MEDIUM ground is found

Moving from center, stretch beyond
BIG, BIGGER, BIGGEST, don't abscond

Be Himalayan Mountains vast
See the whole world happy at last

Take all that love, bring it inside
Put it in your heart to reside

Since Yeti Yawns are contagious
Spread peace, joy, and love courageous

Zoned-In Zebra

There are many PATHWAYS
here on this Earth

Zebras can show you
your heart, strength, and worth

Express the ATTITUDE OF GRATITUDE
It is the key to a positive mood

It doesn't matter if the
road is straight

Get in the zone, reflect,
and make life great

You can choose how you
dance your happy feet

Make them good moves and
enjoy your life's BEAT!

SARAHNDIPITY JOHNSEN danced her
way into this world fully supported
by the grace of her mother. Her
artistic passions continue to grow
and transform through all facets of
Sarahndipity's playful life. As an
award-winner educator and
international entertainer, she delights
in crafting creative programs
designed to inspire and enthuse.
While obtaining her Master's Degree
in Education, a fire lit within her
inspiring *From A-Z: Animals Get
Funky!* and other books, albums,
videos, curriculum, and live events.
Grounding into the expanse of
nature, she loves inspiring
imaginations to take flight through
creative arts. Sarahndipity crafts and
dreams among the Pinyons and
Aspens of Colorado with her
incredible husband and multitudes of
wild, dancing animals.

AMANDA MAITRI was first inspired
in her early childhood by her
Grandmother's stories and
illustrations of Native American
and Inuit tales. She spent countless
hours coloring, and that evolved into
many other artistic endeavors as her
skills and passions grew. The Chicago
art and Hip-Hop scene also had a
major influence on Amanda's craft in
her formative years. She now resides
on the Western Slope of Colorado
where the beauty of nature and life
largely influence her creations.
Using art as meditation, she hopes
her artistic styling continues to
connect others to the divine
beauty within themselves.